BLACKIE the Crow

© 2022 by TGS International, a wholly owned subsidiary of Christian Aid Ministries, Berlin, Ohio.

All rights reserved. No part of this book may be used, reproduced, or stored in any retrieval system, in any form or by any means, electronic or mechanical, without written permission from the publisher except for brief quotations embodied in critical articles and reviews.

ISBN: 978-1-63813-086-4

Cover and text layout design: Kristi Yoder

Printed in China

Published by:

TGS International
P.O. Box 355
Berlin, Ohio 44610 USA
Phone: 330.893.4828
Fax: 330.893.4893
www.tgsinternational.com

BLACKIE the Crow

Written and illustrated by Eva Zimmerman

Introduction

Blackie the Crow is based on a true story about a pet crow that lived near the green meadows years ago. Blackie got into much mischief and could be a real pest at times. But he was a good pet and was friendly to everyone.

—Eva Zimmerman

This story happened years ago, before the Migratory Bird Treaty Act was expanded to include crows. Today it is illegal in the United States to have a wild crow as a pet. The author does not recommend it.

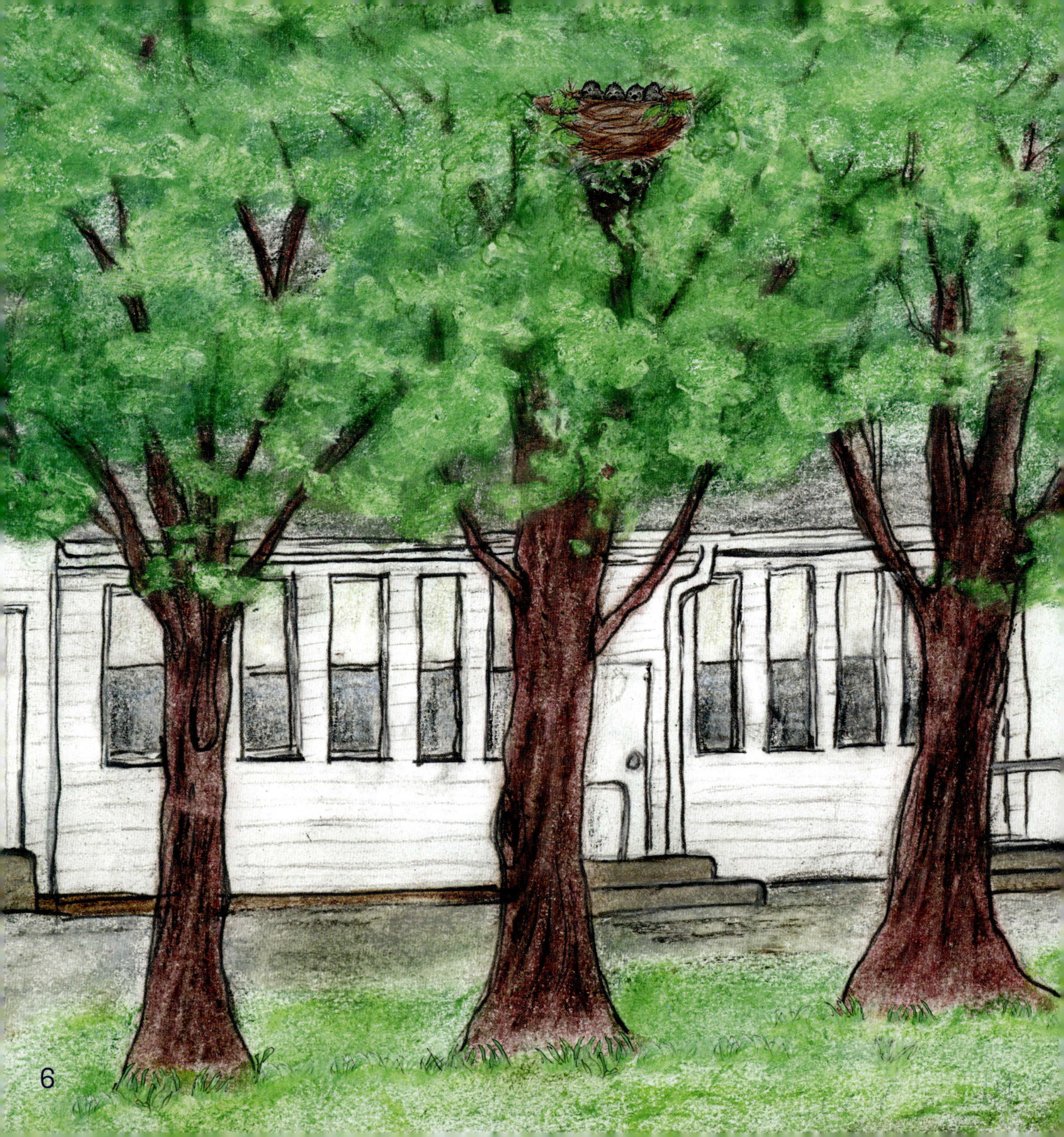

In a little country churchyard, along a little country road, grew a tall, tall maple tree. Way up high in the tree was a big nest made of sticks. In the nest lived Mother and Father Crow and four little baby crows. One of these was Blackie the Crow.

The Crow family was a happy family. Mother and Father Crow flew back and forth bringing food to their hungry babies.

Blackie and his brother and sisters sat in their nest and enjoyed the best view in the whole countryside. Blackie's sharp black eyes didn't miss a thing—not one thing.

He could see the green meadows and all the animals that lived there.

He could see the creek and the woods beyond the creek and all the animals that lived there. He could see all the comings and goings in the churchyard from where he sat in the nest way up high in the tall, tall maple tree.

One night a storm blew in over the green meadows. The wind blew hard, the thunder boomed loudly, and the lightning flashed. The tall maple tree whipped back and forth in the wind. The Crow family huddled down into their nest. Blackie peeped out from under Father Crow's wing. Just then a big gust of wind shook the nest. Poor Blackie fell down, down, down to the ground below! Cold rain drenched Blackie's feathers, and the wind pushed him this way and that. He cawed and cawed, but he could not get back into his nest.

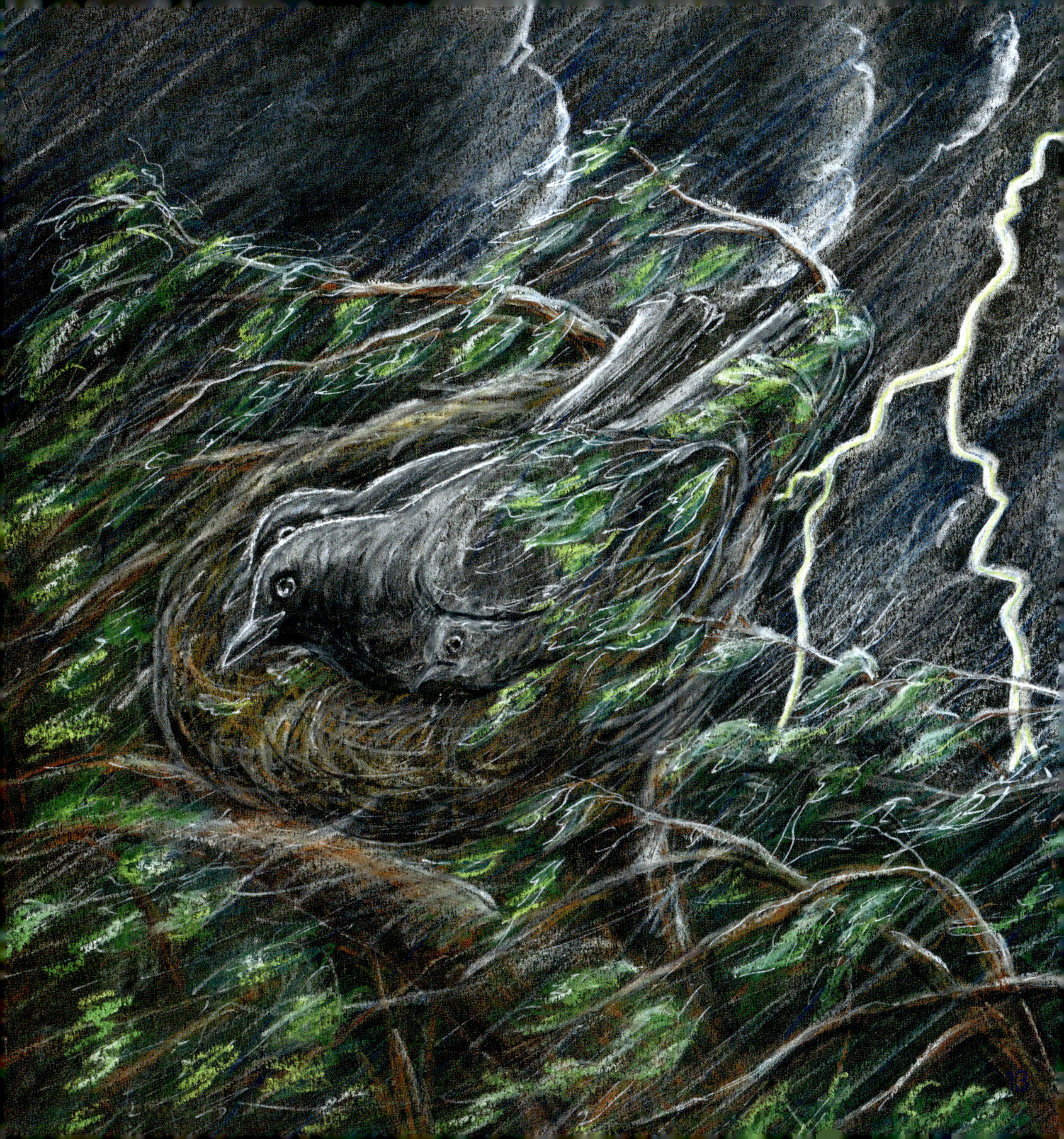

The next morning a man came to clean up fallen branches from the storm. From tree to tree he went until he came to the tall, tall maple tree. There he found Blackie, wet and cold! Gently the man picked him up. He wrapped Blackie in his jacket. Blackie snuggled down in the warm jacket. He felt much better now.

The man took Blackie home to his family. Everyone gathered around. They touched his black feathers. They talked to him in soothing tones. They dried him with a soft towel. Blackie's sharp black eyes watched everything they did. He did not miss a thing—not one thing.

Blackie was hungry. He opened his beak wide and said, "Caw! Caw!" Someone gave him bread soaked in milk. Gulp, gurgle, gulp, down it went. Oh, it tasted good—so good! Again and again he opened his beak wide for more. Blackie liked to eat!

Blackie grew fast in his new home. He learned to know all the family and all the pets. He learned to follow them around and beg for food. He also got into mischief. Oh yes, he did!

Blackie teased Jake the dog. Jake liked to lie on a chair on the porch. Blackie sat on Jake's back and teased him by pulling his hair and nibbling at Jake's ears with his sharp, black beak.

Blackie teased the cats too. When they took a nap in the warm sunshine, he pulled their tails.

When visitors came, Blackie teased the visitors too. He hopped right up on their shoulders or heads and made funny crow noises. How surprised people were when a crow landed on them!

Blackie teased his family too. When they went to the garden, Blackie went to the garden. When they picked beans, Blackie picked beans. But he picked them out of the bucket and dropped them on the ground! He did this just as fast as he could.

The day came when Blackie learned to fly. The trouble was that Blackie learned to fly up but not down. He flew all the way to the top of the tallest tree and cawed and cawed. He wanted his family to come up there and feed him. "Caw! Caw!" he called over and over.

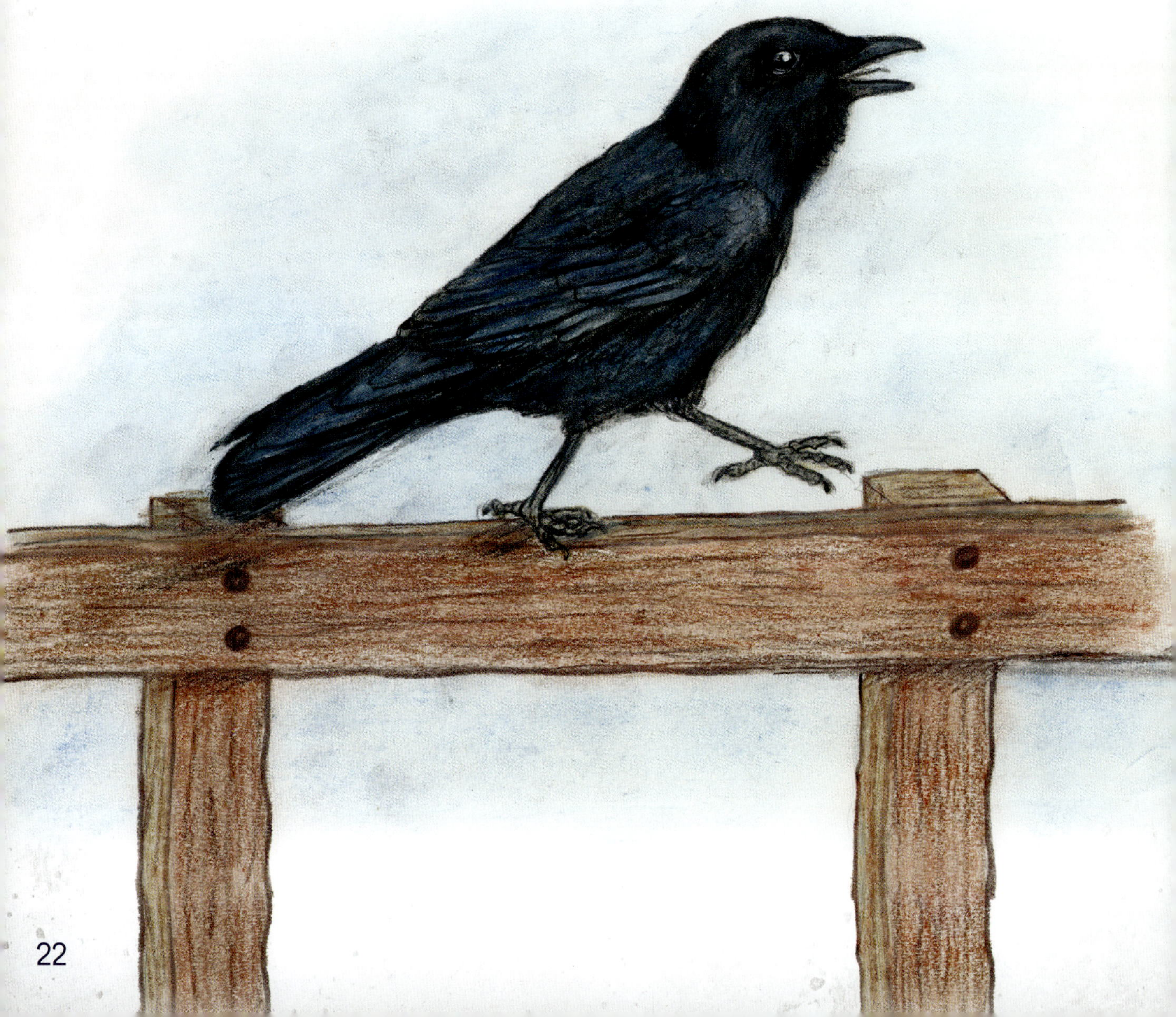

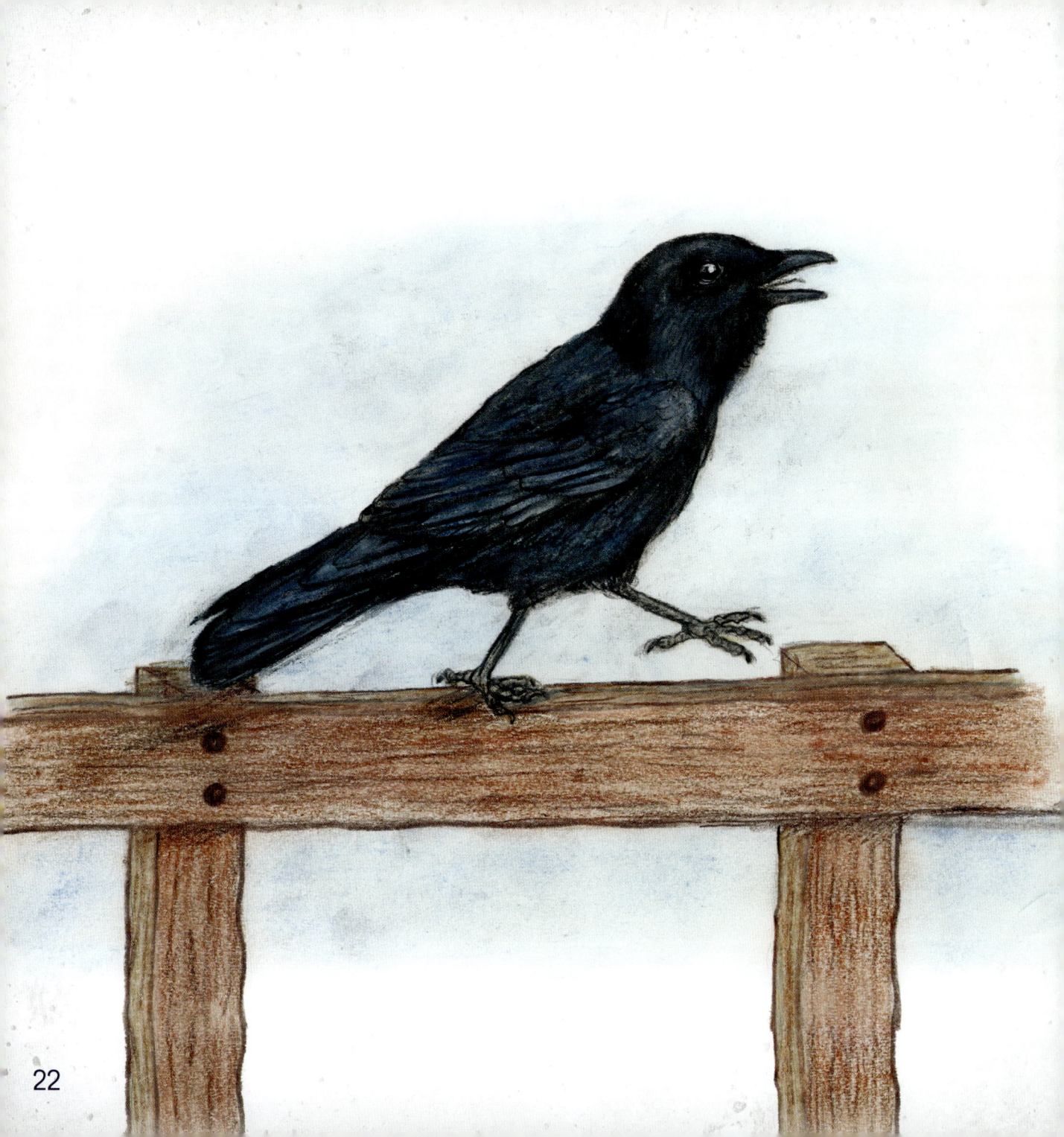

At last Blackie learned to fly down too. Now he could fly up, and he could fly down again whenever he wanted to. He learned to fly so well that he followed the children to school six miles away. High above the road he flew, following the children. When they arrived at school, Blackie arrived at school too and landed on the fence beside them. How surprised they were to see Blackie at school. Blackie cawed softly in happy crow talk. He was very pleased with himself.

Day after happy day went by for Blackie in his new home. Blackie was just a crow, and he went about being a crow just as God had made him.

God made Blackie. He made the birds, the trees, and all the animals. God made everything.

All the animals bring glory to God just by being exactly as God made them.

God also made you. He carefully created you to be His own dear child. You can bring glory to God by being just who He made you to be.

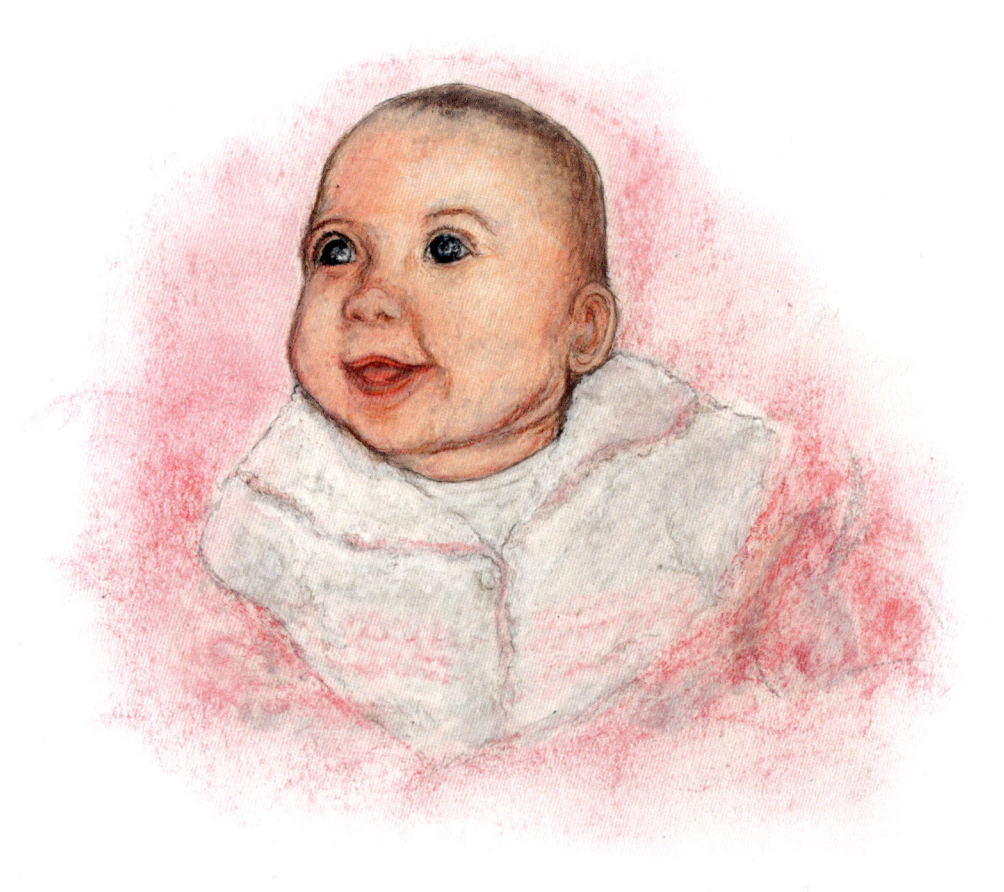

"Thy hands have made me
and fashioned me."
Psalm 119:73

THE END

About the Author

Eva Zimmerman lives in Lancaster County, Pennsylvania, where she taught special education for 25 years. She enjoyed reading picture books to her students.

   She has enjoyed the animals that have lived at her home over the years. Their antics and unique personalities have provided her with many stories to tell.

   Her hobbies include bird-watching, nature walks, drawing, painting, and carving. She also enjoys entertaining children.

   Eva desires to use her talents to the honor and glory of God. She is the author of *Blue Hen and Her Babies*, *Jasper's Secret*, *Little Pony*, *Heather the Sheep*, and *Sam and His Friends* also published by CAM. You can contact Eva by writing to her in care of Christian Aid Ministries, P. O. Box 360, Berlin, OH 44610.

About Christian Aid Ministries

Christian Aid Ministries was founded in 1981 as a nonprofit, tax-exempt 501(c)(3) organization. Its primary purpose is to provide a trustworthy and efficient channel for Amish, Mennonite, and other conservative Anabaptist groups and individuals to minister to physical and spiritual needs around the world. This is in response to the command to "... do good unto all men, especially unto them who are of the household of faith" (Galatians 6:10).

CAM supporters provide millions of pounds of food, clothing, Bibles, medicines, and other aid each year. Supporters' funds also help victims of disasters in the U.S. and abroad, put up Gospel billboards in the U.S., and provide Biblical teaching and self-help resources. CAM's main purposes for providing aid are to help and encourage God's people and bring the Gospel to a lost and dying world.